Food
for Thought

# Food
## for *Thought*

Building Human Capital by Feeding the Mind, Body, and Soul

## CHRISTINE GEORGE

authorHOUSE®

*AuthorHouse™*
*1663 Liberty Drive*
*Bloomington, IN 47403*
*www.authorhouse.com*
*Phone: 1 (800) 839-8640*

*Published by AuthorHouse 07/20/2015*

*ISBN: 978-1-5049-2419-1 (sc)*
*ISBN: 978-1-5049-2379-8 (e)*

*Library of Congress Control Number: 2015911578*

*Print information available on the last page.*

*This book is printed on acid-free paper.*

*I would like to dedicate FOOD FOR THOUGHT to all the hardworking people that do not feel appreciated for coming to a minimum wage job that demands maximum responsibility. To those who are not noticed by their hard work and loyalty, to the single mom that does what she has to do to make ends meet, to the father that accepts jobs when they know it is not enough, and to the one that has an unfavorable background and does not feel that he or she can do better, this is for you.. To the leaders of the company, FOOD FOR THOUGHT will help you communicate and lead employees to go above and beyond what is required of them. If you want to increase or improve the profits in your business, invest in your people.*

*To my friends Akefa and Laketha who weathered the storm with me.*

*To Aubrey, thank you for planting the seed of what a leader should be.*

*And last but not least,*

*to my mother, my husband Patrick, to my two sets of twins; Tierra, Dierra, Jackita, and Larita, and to my grandchildren; that continues to inspire me to be the daughter, wife, the mother, the grandmother, and the woman of God all in one without any regrets.*

# Why Food For Thought?

*FOOD FOR THOUGHT was birthed during a time when employees and leaders of the company where I was employed did not feel worthy, valued, or appreciated. I had to find a way to reach the employees without touching them physically because the company was spread out over several states. I have found that too many businesses are too busy building sales and not building people. Companies are more concerned with numbers and not the people. We must get back to the basics of investing in people and people will invest in our businesses.*

*After working for about 14 years in corporate America, with 12 of those years in leadership, I have had my share of failing as a leader. One of my failing skills was listening to the people; listening even with my eyes. I have always thought I was a good listener, but something happens when you are in charge. You don't have to listen to no one. At least that was what I thought. I had an employee that made me realize this through my own words. I had a quote of the day bulletin board where I put a famous quote or something that "I" felt was important for the employees to read. One day I had "Attitude Reflects Leadership". Well, an employee came to me and asked could she change something on the board. At first I was a little offended because she wanted to change something on "my" board. I "allowed" her to make some changes and she put, "Leadership Reflects Attitude." I thought it was a little redundant at first because it was the same thing, at least I thought it was the same thing. She pointed how she felt directly at me. The Leader. My leadership or the lack of leadership affected her and many others that were under my supervision and I had to make a change and quick. Thanks Krisi for that wake up call.*

*As the Human Resources Director (HRD), I was hired to enhance and protect the bottom line to the company which included the employees. Sometimes it is a moral dilemma of what the company says to do and what we think is morally right. As the HRD, you are the mediator, the motivator, the go- between person, and the intercessor that must find the balance for everyone. I had to listen to the concerns of the people and find ways to encourage employees to continue to come to a job he or she hated by inspiring and motivating them through short stories, testimonies, and poems of laughter and hope for just one more day.*

# Finding the Aubrey in You

Have you ever had that one boss that made you want to do a great job? Have you ever had that one person that made you feel that everything that you did had to be a reflection of how good they were to you? Find your Aubrey! I had the privilege of working for a supervisor that did just that.

Aubrey was the type of guy that made sure you were noticed every day. He started his day by acknowledging each one of his employees by walking down the aisles and speaking to them and asking about their day. He familiarized himself with our family which became his family and his family became ours. He knew our spouses and children by name. He took an interest to know who we were not just for the company's sake, but because it was just who he was. That was his character. He tended to his flock like a shepherd to his sheep. He would know if something was wrong with us and would call us in the office and make sure we were alright. He would also put you in check if you needed checkin'.

Aubrey was the type of guy that had your back. I remember one time the accounting department had been working hard and had not received a bonus for a while. Our department was the only group that received bonuses only if the company made money. Now the other departments received bonuses based on their performances whether or not the company made money. Our bonuses were based off the bottom line and by the time it got to us it was bottomed out! He fought for his team and convinced upper management to give us a hundred dollar bonus. Now, I know you think that is small change, but it depends on whose hand it's in. That hundred dollars was not

1

much, but it was like receiving a million dollars because he cared and he appreciated our hard work. Employees will go above and beyond when they know they can trust you and when they know you will have their back.

When Aubrey had decided to leave the company in 2003, he left me with a book called *"Your Attitude Determines Your Altitude."* I still have this book today. As I managed people throughout the years, this helped me every day to find the Aubrey in me.

Think back to the supervisor or the leader that has had an impact in your life. The one person that made you want to do more without asking. The one person that made you a better employee overall. The one that makes you want to tap, tap, tap…find the Aubrey in you.

# Expecting Something Different?

Every week a pastor would go to church and preach the same sermon Sunday after Sunday. After about the third week, members were complaining and getting angry because they were expecting something different. On the fourth week, once again the pastor began preaching the same sermon again. One of the members stood up and yelled, "Hold on now, for the last three weeks we have listened to you preach the same sermon over and over. Now, we want something different from you today!" The pastor looked at the congregation and stated. "Well, I will preach something different, if you start doing something different!"

The definition of insanity is doing the same thing, but expecting a different result. The preacher only preached the same sermon because he was getting the same reactions, or low or no performances, in return from his members. They were expecting him to preach the sermon, visit the sick, pray for them, and bring the lost souls to Christ. The pastor never reached them because they were not willing to do something different to make an impact. So, if you want different sales, do something different. If you want different quality employees, do something different. So to expect the best results, you will have to start doing something different.

# Are You Directing or Are You Empowering?

Directing is defined as explicit instructions to workers-telling them what to do to meet the goals and objectives of an organization without a voice in the process. Empowering is defined as giving employees the authority to make a decision without consulting the manager. This does not mean employees will make decision based on personal opinion, but empower employees the responsibility to respond quickly to customer requests by complying with the company's policies and procedures with a clear thought process while under the direction of the manager. If managers or the leaders in your company have trained employees properly, this will free up time for managers to concentrate on more cost effective ways that will improve processes and save the company money.

Consider your company's mission statement and if you do not have a mission statement design one that will create an environment of empowering employees. The ultimate end result is to inspire employees to want to become the mission statement not only for the company but also for themselves. So, are you directing or empowering?

# Communication Is Key

Communication is the key to having effective standards implemented properly. It's not so much of what you say, but how you say it. Are your employees listening to you? If you are having problems with an employee (s), he or she are probably not listening. They hear you, but they are not listening. In return, you have to listen to your employees to find out what is needed for them to reach their full potential. Effective communication is a two way street; a person teaching, speaking, training, and another person listening, answering questions, and providing feedback.

An example of using effective communication is in the school when writing papers. If you had a great English teacher, he or she taught you how to write and effective paper by using the 5 W's and sometimes H to communicate your paper; who, what, when, where, why, and sometimes how. I used this writing to tool to implement new processes to help employees understand. This also made it easier for them to answer without thinking that they were actually writing.

An example of ineffective communication is not being honest when asked a question. Now, it is understandable that companies will change things and will not allow any communication regarding the change until everything is confirmed and accepted before making it public. But, not being truthful to an employee creates barriers that are hard to tear down.

For instance, I had been with this particular company for several years and had worked as the supervisor for most of those years. There was a crisis within the company which caused the assistant to the VP job become open. I am very observant and noticed that one of young ladies that I had trained for my department was spending a lot more time with the VP of finance than normal. Keep in mind many of the people that I had trained were picked to move to other departments, but I was asked before they were moved. This particular young lady was very intelligent and she deserved the chance at a promotion, but I had seniority, a degree, and was a supervisor for many years. Everyone in the department was asking me what was going on. I felt bad because I was a senior supervisor and could not give them an answer. I am quite sure they were thinking the same way I was… I should be the next one in line or at least offered the position, or informed of what decision that has already been made. I continued to observe what was going on and noticed that the young lady was cleaning out her files from her current job and informing another employee where the files were.

I decided to go ahead and ask my superior what was going on and was the young lady getting the position. My superior, stated, "No. No decision has been made on who was getting the position." I really was a bit puzzled because I was trying to figure out why the young lady would be moving files and explaining where files were if she had not been given the position or a least thought she was getting the position. Now keep in mind, most of the time when someone ask you a question about something, they pretty much already know the answer. They just want to know whether or not you will tell them the truth. Shortly after our conversation, the announcement was made that the young lady that I had trained had the position that I had inquired about.

After this incident, I could no longer trust anything my boss said, and it caused a serious break in our work relationship. I was not just mad at the fact the young lady got the job and I didn't, but the fact my boss did not trust me enough to tell the truth. Employees just want the truth, whether it's good or bad.

Think about it: do an inventory of your communication technique as a leader and determine if you have effective communication with your employees. Remember your employees are a product of you. Communication is key in building or breaking a relationship.

# 4<sup>th</sup> Quarter!

We are down! You have your coach (CEO, President) and your same starring five players (managers, supervisors, directors). What are you to do? Nothing seem to be going right; running out of products, store marked out of compliance, machines not working, customer complaints, and your sales are down. What are you to do! The coach has to assess the situation and possibly make some player adjustments. No, it's not fun, but necessary. After making the adjustments, the coach has to trust what he has already coached them to do. If the players are not playing the game to win, then why are they playing at all? Why are they on your team? The coach calls the team to the bench to regroup to only hear the blame game being passed on from player to player. The team looks at the coach for leadership….to only find that the coach is not able to handle the stress of being down and out. How will the team ever get back to winning?

1. Get back to the basic fundamentals of the game
2. Train the players to play the game and empower them to add a little to it
3. Focus on improving the weakest areas before moving on to the next step
4. Play as a team and know that you are doing and have done your best; win or lose
5. Know that you are all in this together

Always remember that teams do not make winning coaches, coaches make winning teams! The buzzer has sounded, 4<sup>th</sup> quarter is over! You determine the outcome.

# Lead by Example

As a mother, we train our children not to do certain things for their protection. I had just purchased the iPhone and was excited to begin using it. I had picked up my son from work one day and was driving home. My iPhone vibrated and I picked it up because I had been wanting to really try it out. Well, it was one of my daughters from college and I was texting while driving, about to hit a car, drove in a ditch, and missed a stop sign. You name it, I did it. I was so busy trying out my new iPhone I didn't even think about my son being in the car watching everything that I told him not to do. After my brush with death, he just looked at me and said, "Really, Moma, really?" And I was like, "What did I do?"

The moral of the story is that as a leader we are not exempt from anything. If you are going to lead, then lead. Don't live by these words; "do as I say, not as I do." Ty Bennett, the author of *The Power of Influence*, did a simple test to see how a group of managers and corporate team was listening. He said take your right hand make the ok symbol; now put the circle of your right hand on your chin. Ty asked everyone to do this test at the same time, but to keep their eyes on him. He kept moving his hand closer and closer to his face and his right hand with the ok symbol ended up on his cheek. Then he asked, "how many have the circle on your chin?" everyone looked around and it was about 2 people of out of 50 people that listened to what he said. The rest of us did what he did. You should want your children, employees, or managers to do what you do; if it is conducive with what you are saying.

The mentality of leadership in the workplace should not be, do as I say, not as I do. As a leader you must understand that if you hold your subordinates accountable for their less than acceptable job performance; then you are to hold yourselves accountable as well. Do not accept anything different from yourself, than you would not accept from your employees. If you expect your employees to be at meetings on time; you should be on time. If you expect your employees to follow policies and procedures, you should expect an even higher standard for yourself. You are to lead by example in everything you do. Just because you are in charge, does not make you exempt from any rules.

Everything that you do or do not do is noticed by someone that works with you or around you. You should want your employees to do what you do, if you are leading. Being in charge is a difficult task, but being in charge when no one is looking is an even harder task. Take a look at your leadership style and challenge yourself to be a true leader by leading by example.

# Who Are You Not To Be

In the poem, *"Our Deepest Fear,"* by Marianne Williamson, there are words to live by. The first time I heard this poem was in the movie *Coach Carter.* Coach Carter had a bunch of players no one wanted to work with, but challenged them to believe in themselves further than what they saw in their community or homes. Throughout the movie, the coach asked the players what was their deepest fear. No one knew what he was talking about and didn't seem to care. During the lockout because of the team's failing grades, disobedience, and failure to heed to the warnings of Coach Carter, one particular player stood up and recited the poem in front of the entire team. Then the player stated to Coach Carter that he saved his life. That was pivotal moment in the movie. So, I am asking you, what are you afraid of? Often times you do not reach your full potential not because you cannot do it but you can do it. We will shrink ourselves or lower our standards to fit into the crowd. If you don't fit in the box, don't try it! Build your own box. When you know who are, then your employees will know who they are.

The poem states:

We ask ourselves,
Who am I to be brilliant, gorgeous, talented, fabulous?
**Actually, who are you *not* to be?**

Who are you not be the best manager that you are destined to be?

Who are you not to build the best team possible?

Who are you not to always look for better ways to train, motivate, and promote your employees?

Who are you not to be challenged for you to reach your full potential?

Who are you not to be the undiscovered lion to lead your group above and beyond their expectations?

Today, know that you can be and do anything that you decide that you want to do. Decide today to meet or beat the expectations of your company, personal, and career goals. Everything that you desire to do starts with a thought process, which turns into an attitude or passion, when then it is illuminated into action. I ask you again, who are you to brilliant, gorgeous, talented, fabulous? Actually, WHO ARE YOU NOT TO BE!

# *When you are not there...*

When you are not there, does your work get done or does it wait for you until you come back? When you are not there for a day, will your workplace still operate without you, or it is in a mess when you come back after being gone for a week? When you are not there, are your employees leaving early and are still clocked in? When you are not there, are your employees taking longer lunches than they are supposed to? This all boils down to what are your expectations as a leader when you there and when you are not there. There is no option to think or do anything less than what is expected.

When parents leave children home for the weekend, they expect the children to abide by the same rules as if they were there. *Right?* What normally happen are parents come back home to a home full of people they do not know, furniture is demolished, and cannot find their children. Does that make them a bad parent? No, but it allows the parents to see their expectations were not their children's expectations. But either way, the parents must continue to engrain what is expected into the children so this will never happen again.

Ask yourself these questions on a daily basis until you don't have to ask these questions anymore. Supervisors/Managers should manage the operations of the department, store, or area and not just work their department, store, or area. Directors should manage the operations of their supervisors/managers and not do the work for them. Working in the stores and not managing the stores seems to have become a trend that needs to change because when you are not there...will your company be able to stand?

# Protecting the Brand

Every business should have a statement or slogan that represents the brand of the company. This statement should be engrained into the minds of each leader and passed down to each employee. For instance, as the HR director, I began a slogan after each email that caught on to the company. This statement is what the HR department represented, "to enhance and protect the bottom line to …" This statement represented everything that the HR department was about and everyone understood the purpose of HR. Many of us purchase items because of the brand; Gucci, Louis Vuitton, Prada, Michael Korrs, because of what the brand stands for. When you purchase either one of these brands, you now that you are purchasing top of the line items; quality, the best! In every job you do, you are protecting the brand whether you know it or not.

The quality foods or items you sell, your customer service, clean stores, and hiring good employees can protect the brand you are selling. You are not only selling name brand items, but you are protecting your company's brand. Your company should mean something more than the items that you sell. Do not just think you are selling a brand, but protecting the brand to your company.

# Are you an egg or a coffee bean?

I know many of you are saying to yourself, "What the heck is she talking about?" Ask yourself; are you an egg or a coffee bean? Think about it. Both items are placed in boiling hot water, but have different outcomes. You put an egg in boiling water and the water changes the egg. You have to peel the hard outer shell to find a soft spot, only to realize that the inside is hard too. You put a coffee bean in boiling water and it changes the water. What starts out as clear water, transforms into a different color and gives off a sweet, refreshing aroma that makes everyone want to drink some. Even if they do not like coffee! Coffee smells good and feels good.

As a leader, we are always put in boiling hot situations that cause different outcomes. In your boiling hot situation would you prefer to be the egg or the coffee bean? The egg allowed its surroundings to change it, but the coffee bean changes its surroundings.

So I ask you again, are you an egg or a coffee bean?

# What are you looking at or tell me what you see?

Dr. Myles Munroe wrote in his book, *Power of Vision*, "Eyes that can look are common, but eyes that can see are rare." It took me a minute to figure out the message because ultimately you can reach the same common goal, but you have a different outcome. Two people go to an art gallery and stop by the same exact picture, but come back with two different images of what they have seen. The person that looks at the picture can see what the artist painted, but the person that sees the picture does not only see what the artist painted, but also sees the depth of the picture. They can see joy, anger, sadness, hate, and much more.

In the business world, we often look at problems and do not see opportunities. There is always a bigger picture than what one is looking at. Don't just look at a team that is not working well together, but take the opportunity to develop and build an exceptional team through team building exercises. Don't just look at an employee that has been with your company for 10 years doing the same job, but take the opportunity to see the potential in employees and provide leadership training that will help them to move up in the workforce. Don't just look at an employee that doesn't seem to make it to work on time on a regular basis or seems to be tired all the time. Take the opportunity to modify behavior through coaching and patience and find out the reason why they are late or tired. It might be they can't afford a car or they do not have a babysitter.

Every leader needs to do inventory with each one of their employees and find out what you are looking at and then identify the things that you see within those employees. Now, close your eyes and tell me what you see. WOW! Did you see that? Sometimes not looking so hard or even judging will allow you see. If you do not have a vision of where your company is going, then you will continue to look at problems and not see the opportunities. I ask you again…what are you looking at or tell me what you see?

# If and Then: Conditions and Rewards

Have you heard these words before? I know I have. My mother used it with me and I use it with my children on a regular basis. If…and Then; If I stop eating sweets, then I could lose the weight (LOL). It is all about conditions and rewards. "If" states the condition that clearly acknowledges what needs to be done. "Then" states what you will receive once you have completed your conditions. It is amazing how these two words work hand and hand in completing a task or reaching a goal. These terms are not just bargaining tools, but training tools as well. For instance: if I communicate better with my team, then I can reduce my turnover rate. If I show patience with my team, then we will build team morale and break previous records. If I train my team properly, then I will have better customer service, highest sales ever awards, dedicated employees, and better evaluations. Now, IF you state your conditions, THEN you and your team will reap the rewards.

# Creating the Necessary Environment

Necessary is defined as anything that is essential to achieve a certain result. Anything that is necessary is something that you cannot do or live without to reach certain standards and achieve goals. You need your hear to live, the air to breath, your legs to walk...What is necessary to you? Creating a necessary environment is the difference in being Fortune 500 Company and the company that never makes it.

As you look around your working environment, look over your employees, your existing operations and find out what is necessary to create that environment and do it! Some may have polices, tools, and procedures in place to help create the necessary environment and you choose to make it unnecessary. The hiring process is necessary to recruit the best possible employees. It is necessary to put limitations on expenses to achieve a goal of excellence and to find ways to pay salary increases and provide better benefits. It is necessary to train employees to understand their jobs better. It is necessary that all employees comply with and managers enforce handbook policies and procedures to eliminate possible liabilities. It is necessary for employees to come to work as scheduled and in proper uniform or attire, to keep their jobs and run an effective operation. It is necessary for the leaders in the company to create the necessary environment to be productive. Until you decide that everything that you do is necessary, you have not bought into the mission of moving the company forward. So what are you doing today to make your environment NECESSARY?

# What does being a leader mean to you?

In the book, *The Spirit of Leadership* by Dr. Myles Munroe, leadership is defined as the capacity to influence others through inspiration motivated by a passion, generated by a vision, produced by a conviction, ignited by a purpose. Being a leader has been mistaken as being the person leading the team. Often times, the person leading is not always the person best qualified. A leader can be defined as the person that stays behind and empowers the team to lead or at least seem as if they are leading. Being a leader is someone that is patient, willing to listen, and inspiring. A leader instructs, demonstrates, and releases knowledge to subordinates that will allow growth and enhancement. A leader is humble, not always in the spot light content when someone else is excelling. A good leader is normally the person that no one talks about first or stays behind the scene and watches from a distance while others are exalted. Leadership is a privilege given by the followers that make up their team. Leadership is not a pursuit, but a result. A leader is what the people whom you inspire call you because they aspire to participate in the positive vision that you are presenting to them, whether it is the vision for a country, company, or a cause.

Are you that leader that is willing to go the distance for your team without being noticed? Are you that leader that listens to your employees, understands them, and make them feel like they a part of the vision? Are you that leader of all leaders that understands that being a leader is not always standing in front of the team, but standing with the team? Take the time and define what does being a leader mean to you?

# Training: The Other Vegetable

The purpose of vegetables to the human body is to provide all the vitamins, nutrients, antioxidants, and fibers that are good for you to build a stronger body. A stronger you. Training does, and essentially is the same thing. Training provides knowledge of a job (s) that will increase productivity, boost employee morale, provide a healthy work environment, and develop a strong team! A stronger you. Training helps in developing leadership skills, motivation, loyalty, better attitudes, and other aspects of the job that successful workers and managers usually display. Every company should take the initiative to promote and support training efforts by continually investing in training tools to empower its people. No one wants to do a job without being properly trained, and then be held accountable for things not getting done or not being done properly. An important philosophy for leaders within your company is to crave for training and sell it to your employees to desire the same thing. Just like you want to up sell products to increase sales, up sell your training system and see how your quality in improves; especially customer service. Just remember:

NO TRAINING = NO PERFORMANCE =NO SALES,

LITTLE TRAINING = LITTLE PERFORMANCE = BETTER SALES,

MUCH TRAINING = MUCH PERFORMANCE = THE BEST SALES EVER!

My suggestion to you is to eat and digest training; the other vegetable because it is needed for a healthier balanced team.

# *Everyone Wins!*

My high school Alma Mata, Barbour County Jaguar Varsity boys, ended their 2012 basketball year with a perfect season of 34-0 and a 2-A State Championship title. The coach won Coach of the Year and made it to the Elite 700 club. The leading guard won player of the year. What I admired about these young men is that at the beginning of the year they set their goal to win every game and then exceeded everyone's expectation of winning the state title as well. The team took one game at a time and they did it as a team. It did not matter if they played all year or rode the beach all year; everyone won. For every team, no matter what the product or ball you're selling or playing, there are leaders and followers. This team had a leader that everyone wanted to follow. It did not matter that they were the same age, their focus was bigger than the person leading; it was the vision the leader had that captured their attention. Wherever the player of the year went, the rest of the team wanted to follow because he made them believe they could win every game. Even when it seemed and felt almost impossible to achieve. This young man was eighteen years old and had more vision and passion for a ball than most adults has for his or her current jobs or careers.

To all the managers or leaders in your company, what is your goal that you wish to achieve this year? Sell it to your team, get their buy-in, and watch what happens. Things that you thought could not or should not happen, will happen. If you lead your team the right way, your employees will follow you because everyone wins!

# 100% Customer Satisfaction
## and Nothing Less!

In the book, *The Simple Truths of Service*, by Ken Blanchard & Barbara Glanz, it stated that, "If you do not take care of your customers, somebody is waiting, ready and willing to do it." This book was inspired by Johnny the Bagger.

Johnny is a Down syndrome young man that took his position by storm. Every night he would come home and do a Thought of the Day. His father would type six of these thoughts on one page and print fifty pages each night. That is 300 people that he would impact every time he worked.

When the customers started receiving these little pieces of paper in their bags each day, they would return to the store; day after day. And each time they returned, they would return to the same register where Johnny worked. Now, that is inspirational. Even a bagger can make a difference.

Many companies have a rating system done by its corporate office, employees, customers, or by franchises. Customer satisfaction is a particular area that companies are rated on that may affect a lot of its bottom line. As a standard, the customer should be the single most important factor in having a successful business----without customers, your business does not exist. Every individual that comes in your establishment is your customer, whether you know them or not, you are the difference between making a positive impact that will make the customer want to come back to your business one more time or a negative impact that will allow that customer and many others not to want to come back ever again. No business exists without great customer service.

Companies must remember that your competitive edge is not just the quality of your product, or how fast your service is, and not even your prices; it is "how you treat your customers". Expect 100% customer satisfaction from every employee that makes up your company and nothing less.

# Facing the Giant

Some of you may have seen the movie called *"Facing the Giant"* and some of you have read the biblical story about David and Goliath. These are stories to depict the image of the weakest versus the strongest or the underdog overcoming unbelievable obstacles and triumphs and defeating the odds. The fear of not knowing what to expect is sometimes the underlying factor that delays progress. To give you some insight of what fear really is here is an acronym: **F**antasized **E**xperiences **A**ppearing **R**eal. We sometimes make the giant bigger that it really is.

When there are new systems that are implemented by your company, they tend to become larger than one can imagine and more of a problem than an accomplishment. For instance, implementing a new training system to find out no one is actually using the system. Your service and sales are affected. Employees are unhappy because they do not know what the heck they are doing and customers are frustrated because they know the employee do not know what they are doing. So now the easy training system has a much larger negative impact than what was planned. No one plans for the Giant! Often times the Giant will have you convinced that you can defeat it, but never why you should defeat it. The Giant will take you out of to make you think outside of the box. The Giant will make you tap into the inner self you never knew and make you become the leader that you never met.

In the movie, the underdog team defeated the giant team and the biblical story, David defeated Goliath. Whether it is implementing a training system, creating a policy manual, or whatever it may be, it will not defeat you but only unleash the type of leaders that is already within you. Stand up and Face your Giant!

# Consistency Doesn't Lie

Being consistent can be described as something being reliable or in agreement with. For instance, you can consistently wake up at the same time every day or consistently wear your hair the same way. But just like anything else, consistency has a negative or a positive effect. If you find that you are consistently doing things the right way, the wrong way, or doing things your own way regardless which way is right or wrong, consistency doesn't lie. If you are consistently driving to increase your sales and shooting to lower wasteful use, consistency doesn't lie. If you are holding employees accountable for not doing their jobs, consistency doesn't lie. If you are training according the manual, consistency doesn't lie.

One thing I do know consistency will show in numbers, in the attitude of your employees, and most of all in leadership. Consistently speaking positively about changes or improvements within the company, consistently improving the atmosphere of your work environment, consistently challenging and motivating your team to do and be the best they can be. If you do or if you don't...Consistency doesn't lie!

# Leading by Fear or Leading by Inspiration

How are you leading your team by fear or by inspiration? I know some of you are saying, "What is she talking about?" Example: When you are in your team's presence, are they unhappy, nervous, forgetful, non-communicative, and running around like a chicken with its head cut off? If so, then you are leading by fear. Or, when you are in your team's presence are they happy, diligently doing their tasks with ease, communicating with no problems or even asking questions. If so, then you are probably leading by inspiration.

Each leader in a department, store, or company needs to take note of the action of your employees in your presence. If you are leading by fear, it can be a debilitating mechanism that makes you an ineffective leader.

Often times a person in authority leads by fear because they are ineffective and do not want anyone to see their short-comings. Leading by inspiration is a tool used to allow employees to willingly want to go above and beyond their job because of how it benefits them as well as the team.

Communicate to your team in an inspiring fashion without any regrets of what was said or how it was said. Inspire them to become more diligent employees. Respect them by listening and not be the criticizing hand that puts the employee in a position to not communicate to you at all.

I challenge you to not lead by fear because it only benefits you or your ego. If you are leading by fear, your employees are glad to see you go and stop working when you leave. If you are leading by inspiration, your employees understand that you leave them with tasks to complete and they are still working well after you have left. Do inventory of your leadership skills and ask yourself… How am I leading; by fear or inspiration?

# Value Added

Value added is defined as the enhancement a company gives it product or service before offering the product to the customers. As I think of value added I think of it a little different way. My definition of value added is the enhancement that you give to your company that is presented before your customers, vendors, and employees. *You* are the value added!

In everything that you do, you are a very important part of how things are done within the company. McDonald's does not have Big Mac without the value of the special sauce added to the sandwich. For any company, there is not business without the value of a leader added to make a difference in the development of their team to increase sales, boost employee morale, and to have great customer service. There is no growth without the value of changing the mentality of your people added to become the best in every level of your company. A company does not have the value of the people added which makes the difference in who you are to customers, vendors, and to each other. Your company is the best because *you* are the Value Added.

# Standard or Optional?

Standard is an acceptable behavior, policy, procedure, or process in which you allow to happen on your job or in your life. An option could be the decision that you make to do or not to do within the standards set before you. I know in my home I have standards. No dishes left over night, keeping your room clean and do not leave the toilet seat up may be a few of standards that you may have in your homes. In my home, I have one that everyone must abide by or there will be a price to pay. Everyone knows if there is only one Coca-Cola in the house, it belongs to me! This is not an option. I know some may think this is a little extreme, I have high expectations or this is even funny, but that is my standard. In my professional life, I like my desk clean and everything put in its place or finds a place for it. My thought process is, when clients come into my office, she knows what she is doing, or at least they think I know what I am doing (LOL). Everything must have a label. This makes my office user friendly for anyone that needs to find something in my office; they will be able to find it.

When creating standards it is passed on from person to person no matter the circumstances are or what you are doing. If you make something optional, you take the chance of something not being passed down from person to person. Oh better yet, it is time for dinner and I do not have my Coke!! This means that something will get left out or not done because you allowed the optional to become your standard.

It should be standard for us to follow processes for your organization to be productive to meet or beat sales expectations from one week or month to the other, train and development a successful team, and have the absolute best service for our customers every time. Once you allow your standards to become optional you are not able sustainable in a competitive market. If you allow your standards to become optional, your employees are not doing their hired responsibilities, and then you will not meet your sales expectations. You will possibly receive customer complaints instead of customer compliments. If you allow simple day to day routines and tasks to be overlooked, you have just made the company standards optional. Every policy, rule, or report are standards created by the company and for the company's benefit as well as the employee's benefit. As a leader in the company, have you made necessary procedures; Standard or Optional?

# Identify Who You Are and Walk In It!

Being a mother of two sets of twins, can be a difficult job. In 2011, my daughters played basketball for a junior college. One of my daughters was almost kicked off the team because of her attitude. As a little girl growing up, I knew she was bigger than life could handle at times, but never to the point that her coach was not going to tolerate. The coach contacted my husband and me and we made a Sunday trip to the school. You know it was trouble! We missed church! The reason she was almost sent home was because she allowed her helping and listening to people's problems to become her problems. Therefore, she became like the person she was helping. She was no longer influencing, she was *being* influenced. The one thing that I have always taught my children, "Don't follow the crowd. Lead the way because that is who you are." It is in their DNA! Her feelings were no longer her feelings; she was feeling like the negative young lady she befriended. Her thoughts were no longer her thoughts; she began to think like her friend. She no longer identified with who she was. Nothing changed about the game, nothing changed about the coach, and nothing changed about her teammates. The only thing that changed was her. She could not identify with that. It was her against everyone else.

In 2012, the coach allowed her to come back another year to play for him. It was a difficult decision, but he knew the young lady that he recruited was not the young lady he had seen the last couple of months. This year was totally different. Instead of the coach contacting my husband and me to kick her off the team, he was calling to inform us how much our daughter meant to him because of her leadership. He stated that he had the best team he had ever coached and felt that it was because of the direct reflection of my daughter's leadership. She finally got the team to follow her, instead of her following her team member. The power of influence affects a magnitude of people! (Did I mention the young lady that was a negative influence on my daughter was not called back to the team a second year?)

In Ty Bennett's book, *The Power of Influence,* he speaks on five applications of influence: 1. Develop Outward Thinking, 2. Investing In People, 3. Focus on Being Interested, Not Interesting, 4. Practice the Platinum Rule, and 5. Seek to Serve. Applying these five concepts will build a better team and create a better leader.

Often times in leadership, we try to fit in with the crowd to convince subordinates to like us. It is not your job to have them to like you, but it is their job to respect you and your position. As a leader you want the people working with you to like you and I totally understand that, but your presence and character will do that on its own. You will not have to do anything extra for that. Be careful of compromising your position as a leader to fit in. For instance fraternizing with employees in which a friendship is created and not knowing authority boundaries. Having an employee as your friend is not a problem, but when a leader is not able to separate the two and jeopardizes his/her authority over that friend and create a hostile working environment with the other employees, then it is a problem. Just do your job consistently in a fair approach for all employees and they will like you and respect you. But, until you identify who you are in your own skin and your own thoughts, then you are unable to influence people to follow you. Once you do, you are now able to bring about a change, a shift in improving people, to modify behavior, or promote; ultimately, to make a difference. So identify who you are and walk in it!

# The Lost Lion

In Dr. Myles Munroe book, *The Spirit of Leadership*, he tells a story about a "Lion Among Sheep". In this story, a lion cub is left by its parents and a farmer finds the lost lion and takes it back to the farm and raise it among his sheep. The lost lion was accepted by the sheep. The lost lion slept, grazed, and became a sheep by association.

In this particular story, the sheep could not teach or lead the lost lion on how to be a lion; only how to be another sheep. Sheep are not leaders. They are followers by nature. How many of you believe that a sheep cannot lead a pack of lions, but a lion can lead a pack of sheep? Lions are leaders by nature. They are the king of the jungle. Not by association, but by belief. Everyone in the jungle know that the lion is the king and the lion do too.

How many lost lions do you have working in your company? Are you a lost lion by association? I can relate to this because I was in an accelerated reading class when I was in the 5th grade with nothing but Caucasian boys. The teachers thought I would not do well in the class because I was the only African American girl. So, they placed me in a remedial reading class. Keep in mind I was an accelerated reader, but I became a slower reader because I associated myself with the students in the class. I was lost! I eventually returned to the accelerated reading class, but only because I was lead out of the class. The teacher of the remedial reading class noticed that I could pronounce harder words, more so than the rest of the class. She realized I did not belong in the class before I did.

So many employees does not belong in their positions because they are lost. Often times, a lost employee will not want to become a leader or a manager because they associate themselves with the sheep in the company; the followers. They hate to leave the safe, secure, and simple place to venture out to unpredictable, unsure territory in fear of something. In fear of failing or losing the followers, better yet in fear of realizing they can really do the job.

As a leader, it is your responsibility to find the lost lions in the workplace and place them in their rightful positions. Empower them to find their true self and embark on the territory they were born to do. Now, go find your lost lion!

# The True Character in You

In a particular professional development meeting on leadership training, the word character came up several times in the group conversations. The reason is, you cannot speak on leadership without speaking on a man's character. Dr. Martin Luther King, Jr. stated that, "The ultimate measure of a man is not where he stands in moments of comfort and conveniences, but where he stands at times of challenges and controversy."

Character is the action you take to carry out the values, ethics, and morals that you believe in. Character is your make-up. It is who you are. It is the consistency between what you say you will do and what you actually do. It is putting your ethics into action. Your character defines, shapes, or breaks your reputation. Your character is your moral strength. It takes moral courage to do what is right when it may cost more than you are willing to pay. Your character defines who you are even if no one is looking. Dr. King is the epitome of what character is in his journey that cost his life.

Your leadership is your character. Your character is what influences people to follow you through moments of discomfort and inconvenience. As a leader, you will have many challenges and controversies that will define who you really are. Everyone can seem to do well when everything is going right, but when things go wrong, everyone will see the true character in you.

# *How many of you believe that?*

Reflection is a productive way to see what has been done throughout the year in a relationship or company. Reflecting on what has changed and what needs to be changed to be an effective person or business. Convincing your team to believe in you and your vision can be a difficult task. How many of you believe that? As a leader you must implement creative tactics to put your beliefs into action. One thing that I do know is that no one will do anything that he/she does not believe in. A thief does not steal unless he believes he can get away with it. A child will not ride their first bicycle without the training wheels unless he or she believes they can do it. An entrepreneur will not open their first business unless he or she believes many years down the road they would be successful. Employees will not follow their leader unless they believe in what the leader is trying to accomplish.

Putting your belief into action should be a way of life. Joyce Meyers has a poem in her book *Power Thoughts*, will help you keep beliefs in prospective.

Watch your thoughts, for they become your words.
Watch your words, for they become your actions.
Watch your actions, for they become your habits.
Watch your character, for it becomes your *identity.*

Whatever you believe you will put it into action; no matter if it is negative or positive. If you believe in your mission statement, you will put it into action. If you believe in your company's policies and procedures, you will put it into action. Let me tell you what I believe.

I believe that your company is greater than what you see. I believe your managers or supervisors have great potential and with a little more time you will have a company full of leaders. Those leaders are intelligent people that can make your largest impact in your company. Most of all, I believe the best is yet to come. How many of you believe that?

# A Diamond in the Rough, How Far are you willing To Dig?

How far are you willing to dig to find your diamond? In fine jewelry the phrase "diamond in the rough" is metaphorical and relates to naturally occurring diamonds that are quite ordinary at first glance, and that their true beauty as jewels is only realized through the cutting and polishing process. A diamond in the rough is found approximately 85 to 120 miles deep into the ground before its value is emerged.

In the business world, we can relate to this phrase to someone that has hidden exceptional characteristics and/or future potential, but currently lacks the final touches that will add value. So how far are you willing to dig for your diamond in the rough? We all have value, some more than others, but a diamond in the rough takes a little more time and effort to see the true value and beauty that has not yet surfaced. True Leaders recognize their diamonds. The leaders realize that it is not always the one that is hitting the targets all the time, it is not the one that is showing up and showing out all the time, but it is the one that makes the front runner looks good. It might be that assistant that is content being an assistant, the mail or errand person that is content running errands, or just another employee trying to just make ends meet that has been at the same position for the last five years making the same pay and will not complain. These are your diamonds. This is the time to start digging!

A diamond is not going to shine on its own; it will need a little help from you; cutting and polishing until all the rough edges are a thing of the past. Encouraging words, a smile, a pat on the back, or even a little eye contact for assurance will make the difference on whether you have a diamond on the front show case or the ones that are in the back. The location makes a difference in the value of your diamond. Jewelry stores take care of its fine diamonds and realize its value way before it is presented and you should too.

Dig deeper to find your diamond. You might have to have some one-on-one time with your employees to find out their likes and dislikes. Dig deeper and cut away things that are holding employees back from excelling that has nothing to do with the job but everything to do with them. Find your diamond in the rough in every employee that works for you until your company reeks of value, power, and prestige. Seek out the potential in your people and start digging for your diamond in the rough.

# "Attitude Reflect Leadership.. Captain"

In the movie, "Remember the Titans," starring Denzel Washington, was a pivotal time where change was happening whether they liked it or not. In Alexandria, Virginia in 1971, the school board was under a federal mandate to integrate an all-black school with an all-white school. T.C. Williams High School, home of the mighty, mighty Titans football team, had to endure a change that put the entire community to a test.

This is the first time some of these students of different color and backgrounds had to co-mingle together. Let alone, play football together. In the midst of integrating the school, the board also decided to take Coach Yoast, the current head white coach down and place Coach Boone, played by Denzel Washington, as the new head black coach of the formerly known all-white high school. This is just too much to digest in one day! Could you imagine this time in 1971 when all these changes were made and you just had to deal with it? There was anger, hate, and chaos throughout the town.

One of the most memorable times in the movie is when Julius, the black athlete confronts Gerry Bertier, the white team captain regarding his leadership skills. Coach Boone had the entire staff to attend football camp. Julius was the chosen black football leader and Bertier was the chosen white football leader. They both had a part in making this team work together as one. Although they were playing on the same team they were still segregated. The white players would block for the white players and the black players played as if they were the only ones on the team; not acknowledging the whites as being part of the team. The blacks did what they wanted to do for their black team members and the whites did what they wanted to do for their white team members. At this particular time, Coach Boone had the guys going for three-a-day practices because they were asked to get familiarized with each player of a different race each week and report back to him. Until each player had done so, the team went to three-a-day practices. This was killing the guys. So, while going to the water cooler after a long hard day of practicing, Julius and Bertier both ended up at the cooler at the same time. Bertier stood and looked at Julius and said, "Ok, let's get some particulars out of the way. I Gerry, you are Julius?" During this conversation Gerry complimented Julius about having "wasted talent" and further criticized Julius about not doing his job. Then Julius asked Gerry, "So you are the captain, right and you have been doing your job, right? Gerry said with confidence, "Yes, I have been doing my job." Julius then stated, "If you have been doing your job, why haven't you gotten on your white buddies about not blocking for Rev. They have not been blocking for Rev worth a blood nickel and you know it! And I suppose to kill myself for the team? What team? For now own, I am going to be looking out for me and mine." Gerry looked at Julius with disappointment and stated; "Now that's just the wrong attitude." Julius said, "Attitude Reflects Leadership, Captain."

Often times as leaders, you do not look at yourself as the problem maker, but more of the problem solver. Your team is a *reflection* of you. If your team is not doing their best, you need to check yourself first and then your team. You have to ensure you are providing everything needed for your team to be successful in what he or she does. Your actions, your conversations, your daily demeanor affects your team on a day-to-day basis. Julius had his faults, but he had to make sure Gerry knew where it stemmed from. So don't get mad when your employees call you out. Own it, correct it, and make a difference in yourself as well as in your team. Once you own your faults you can make a change.

Once Gerry knew the truth about himself, as the captain of his ship; he brought about a change to himself and to his team. They were no longer a segregated team. They became the T.C. Williams High School Titan Football Team which was undefeated for the season. Attitude does reflect leadership. The attitude of the players was the true attitude of the captain. In the beginning, Gerry did not want the black players on "his" team. The team was okay without "them" without even saying the words; his actions spoke loudly and made Gerry an ineffective leader.

Bishop T. D. Jakes stated, "Don't Lead Beyond Your Own Exposure." Gerry had not been a leader in this type of environment before. As a leader you have to be careful of the attitude your project to your team because a lot of toxic behaviors can be developed because of it. Group clicks, bad attitudes, and an unproductive employee which will develop an ineffective team. A leader helps to develop, helps to grow, and helps to produce better employees. Are your actions, standards, and attitude conducive to your leadership? Remember, Attitude Reflect Leadership, Captain.

# Don't Let No One Take You Out of Your Game

The 1992 U. S. Olympic National Team better known as "The Dream Team" consisted of Charles Barkley, Larry Bird, Clyde Drexler, Patrick Ewing, Magic Johnson, Michael Jordan, Christian Laettner, Karl Malone, Chris Mullin, Scottie Pippen, David Robinson, John Stockton and Chuck Daly, the coach. This was the best collaboration of basketball talent ever! The biggest names in basketball history united. Old school meets new school. Expectations demanded from all members. As good as this team sound, they still had issues. When you have a team of this caliber, where everyone is an A employee or player, it seem like it should be easier to work together. NOT! These types of teams are often times the most difficult to collaborate, to lead, or even play together.

Watching the *30 for 30* documentary about the Dream Team, I realized there were a lot of egos. Although many of the players knew each other, on and off the court, everyone wanted to shine at this particular time. Everyone wanted to be the MVP. We all know that basketball players better yet most athletes are trash talkers. Trash talking is a player's tactic to get their opponents out of their game. It appears that Magic Johnson was gunning for Michael Jordan.

During the scrimmages, all you could hear was Magic Johnson challenging the players, mainly Michael, on how he was going to school them. Michael was mostly calm and focused. Magic continuously talked trash about what he was going to do. Michael never made a comment. Actually, Michael was very humble and respectful because Magic was a phenomenal player. Magic had made a name for himself. There was nothing that Michael could have done to take away from what Magic had already accomplished. In a particular game, Michael was team captain and Magic was the team captain. It came a point where it appeared that no one was playing the game but Magic and Michael. The other team members basically cleared the path for a one on one game. This was bound to happen. Once the game was over, Michael entered the locker room and looked at Magic and stated, "There is a new sheriff in town." Magic could only give Michael his respect.

What I have learned in leading, supervising, or managing people is that it is enough room for everyone to be seen, if you have room to share the space. When people talk loud or over talk you, it is really fear; fear of not knowing what their opponent will do or capable of. When people talk loud, let them talk. Often times, people or your competition who talks loud is trying to cover up their short comings. You know what you capable of. You are in control. Your presence does not take away from another person's capabilities or accomplishments. Magic was just being Magic and wanted the show for himself and did not have the space to share, but when the game was over and Michael's team won, he had to realize that he could move over a little and share the spot light. No matter what your trash talking opponent says or even does to you, don't let no one take you out of your game.

# Lose To Win

American Idol, Fantasia Barrino, wrote a song called Lose to Win. Some people cannot understand the concept of losing something and winning at the same time. In her video, she was losing her love interest to win herself. Often times we tend to lose ourselves in a man, woman, or even our jobs to feel complete. She made a life changing decision to choose herself by losing him and winning her.

My daughters are athletes and I use sport scenarios because there is so much to learn from an athletic analogy. In one of their games, they lost and one of my daughters complained about everyone else. I had listened to her vent about how they wouldn't pass the ball, they weren't hustling, they didn't want it bad enough, and that the coach wouldn't take a player out who was making a lot of mistakes. As I listened, I asked her, "What did you learn from losing the game?" She looked at me like I wasn't listening. See, there is always a benefit or something to learn when you have lost something or someone. Because anytime you lose it is not a time to blame, but a time of reflection. You just have to take the time out and stop and listen for the lesson. In the words of Katt Williams, "Wait for it, Wait for it." This was the time to reflect back on her and not everyone else and find out how she could have made a difference in the game. What could have been done to change the outcome from losing the game to winning the game? If you do not reflect, you will miss the lesson. That is why coaches always go back to the films to see what could have been done differently to change the outcome or to improve. Keep in mind some coaches are not always just looking at the players, I believe they also look at themselves to see how they can help the players. As a leader in a company, when sales are not met, don't just always look at the team to see why they hadn't met their goals, because they are your goals too. Find out what you could have done to help them reach their sales and come up with corrective actions to achieve goals.

After looking at me for a while and probably thinking, "Why is she asking me this question?" I don't want to hear her. I am mad and it's their fault." She took a deep breathe, and said...wait for it... "I could have done better. I should have stayed focused on trying to help the team and not focused on why they didn't pass the ball." We miss valuable lessons not looking at the bigger picture; not putting things into perspective. Losing is not always bad. It hurts but you should always learn something about yourself from the loss. Losing someone/something pushes you to higher limits. Losing helps one to reach their full potential in many cases. You may lose someone to win your purpose in life. I lost my brother in 2005 and won my motivation. I was more determined to accomplish my goals that he was not able to accomplish. That loss pushed me to my full potential. You may lose an employee to win your self-respect and to win a team back as well. You may lose a challenge to win your identity. You may lose a game to win your self-confidence. You may lose a job to win your family, your career, and peace of mind.

No one enjoys losing anything, but everyone enjoys winning something. Sometimes that is the only way to truly find your purpose, your potential, your reason for being; your worth. Sometimes you gotta lose to win again.

# This Time Next Year

In 2014, I attended a Women's Retreat in Panama City, Florida that changed my life forever. The theme of the retreat was *"Withholding Nothing"*. It was phenomenal! This was the second retreat that I had ever attended. There were six to seven selected women of God that would speak on a topic that was given to them. All the women were great speakers and had powerful messages, but this particular speaker, Evangelist Kecia Evans spoke to me and her message convicted me and changed my life. I really don't remember her topic, but I do remember her message; "This Time Next Year."

In her message, she began to speak boldly to the women and opened up a flood of what will be happening to us, this time next year. She stated that this time next year, you will be an evangelist. This time next year you will be a lawyer, a doctor, a pastor, and business owners. This time next year you will be an author! I almost fell out of my chair. I stood up with tears rolling down my face. She continued to speak and I continued to listen. She stated that many of us had words in our minds that needed to be put on paper. I knew she was talking to me because I had been told by several people to put Food for Thought into a book and I did not listen, but I was listening now.

In Romans 4:17, "As it written, I have made thee a father of many nations, before him whom he believed, even God, who gives life to the dead, and calls those things which do not exist as though they did." This speaker spoke life into the women that were dead. She spoke our future back into our lives. Sometimes we need someone to just speak to us to bring us back to reality or life. This should be the same way with your child, friend, spouse, or employee. When you have a mediocre child not living up to their full potential, tell them about this time next year. I told one of my twin sons that he was going to be a barber and that he was going to have his own business with his brother. I purchased the chair, just waiting on the business. When you have a friend that seems to keep making the wrong mistakes, tell them about this time next year. When you have a spouse that is not living up to their part of the relationship, tell them about this time next year. When you have an employee that is mediocre and you know he/she is a leader, tell them about this time next year! Continue to engrain faith, until a change comes. Never give up; never give in because you will not be the same child, friend, spouse, or employee this time next year!

Message to Employers:

Employees must feel value deeper than your pockets and higher than a promotion. If an employee's presence or worth is not valued, your employees will show their value and their worth through poor customer service, insubordination, and/or theft. All of which causes loss in the company's sales and ultimately loss in profits. Remember you probably were in their shoes before. It is everyone's responsibility to enhance and protect the bottom line to your business. So, always listen to the signs. Leadership or the lack of leadership is a huge part of why employees act the way they do. I recommend Ty Bennett's book, *The Power of Influence* to get you started on how important your leadership or the lack of leadership influences your employees on a day-to-day basis.

Message to Employees:

Continue to do the expected as well as the unexpected even if you are not noticed or rewarded by your superiors. Someone will notice when you least expect it. Stay focused, stay honest, and stay loyal. It will get you as far as you are willing to go. Stay positive. Olympic gold medalist Scott Hamilton had said, "The only disability in life is a bad attitude." Nothing will hinder or handicap you in life as severely as a bad attitude. When using the word attitude, I am referring to the system of thoughts, the mental posture, the mind-set, or the way of thinking with which a person approaches life. So don't focus on the negative things in your life or the negative things that have happened to you, but focus on the positive things in your life and the positive things that are going to happen for you. If you are not sure where to start, I recommend you reading Steve Harvey's book, *Act Like a Success, Think Like a Success.* This book will start you on a way to re-inventing yourself to a better you.

# Power Thought

This was an amazing journey to complete this book and I am very thankful that it's done. I thank God for allowing me to be a vessel to help change people way of thinking through inspiration. Many times I felt that it was not worth it, it was too time consuming, and nothing would become of it. Keep in mind, everything you are reading in this book I was using to encourage others, but I was the one that was in need of encouragement.

One of my favorite poems is *"Our Deepest Fear"* by Marianne Williamson. I love this poem because it describes what I have been doing for years. She states in her poem, "Your playing small does not serve the world. There is nothing enlightened about shrinking so that other people will not feel insecure around you." For so long I have shrunk to fit in. I have shrunk to ensure that people liked me. I have shrunk and not show what I am really capable of because I did not want to upset anyone or make them feel like I was taking over. So what! Let them think that. No more sitting back and watching or using the excuse that I am "observing".

My message to everyone that is reading this book is to never give up. It is never too late to live your dream out loud! Things may seem that it is not working in your favor. Things may seem like it's always harder for you. But I encourage you to fight for the passion that burns inside of you. Just know God is working behind the scene. Everything that has happened to you and is going to happen to you is a divine order for your purpose. In Proverbs 29: 18 states, "Where there is no vision, the people will perish." If you do not have a vision for your company, your employees, or even your life, ***you will perish***. You must have a vision further than your present state. No matter how bad it appears to be. My vision was to write a book and I did it and you can, too!

# *Inspirational Food for Thought Quotes:*

*You must become the change you desire to see in the world.*

**-Mahatma Ghandi**

*It is better to lead from behind and to put others in front, especially when you celebrate victory when nice things occur. You take the front line when there is danger. Then people will appreciate your leadership.*

**-Nelson Mandella**

*Leadership is the capacity to influence others through inspiration motivated by a passion, generated by a vision, produced by a conviction, ignited by a purpose.*

**-Dr. Myles Munroe**

*You don't need a title to be a leader.*

**-Multiple Attributions**

*Leaders do not follow path-they create trails. They venture where others don't dare to tread.*

**-Dr. Myles Munroe**

*People buy into the leader before they buy into the vison.*

**-John Maxwell**

*Leadership is a privilege given by followers.*

**-Dr. Myles Munroe**

*No man will make a great leader who wants to do it himself, or to get all the credit for doing it.*

**-Andrew Carnegie**

*The challenge of leadership is to be strong, but not rude; be kind, but not weak; be bold, but not bully; be thoughtful, but not lazy; be humble, but not timid; be proud, but not arrogant; have humor, but without folly.*

**-Jim Rohn**

*Trapped within every follower is an undiscovered leader.*

**-Dr. Myles Munroe**

*A leader has to remember that people tend to follow the leader's actions. You can't say one thing and do another and expect people to believe in you or follow you. As the leader, you have the opportunity to set an example of how the business should be run.*

**–David Novak**

*A leader is what the people around you inspire to call you because you participated in the positive vision that you are presenting them, whether it is the vision for a country, a company, or a cause.*

**–Dr. Myles Munroe**

# Notes:

Bennett, Ty (2010). *The Power of Influence: Increase Your Income and Personal Impact.* www.soundconcepts.com.

Blanchard, K., Glanz, B. (2005). *Simple Truths of Service. Inspired by Johnny the Bagger.* www.simpletruths.com

Daily Bread Ministries. www.ourdailybread.org

Meyers, Joyce (2010). *Power Thoughts: 12 Strategies to Win the Battle of the Mind.* www.faithword.com.

Munroe, Myles Dr. (2003). *Power of Vision: Keys to Achieving Personal and Corporate Destiny.* www.whitakerhouse.com

Munro, Myles Dr. (2005). *The Spirit of Leadership: Cultivating the Attitudes that Influence Human Action.* www.whitakerhouse.com.

Perry, Millicent (2005). *Fe-mails. eCelebration of Women One Click at a Time.* www.iuniverse.com.

# *About the Author*

Christine George has fourteen years of combined experience in corporate finance, human resources, and leadership training. She specializes in professional and personal development. After obtaining her bachelor's in business marketing and her master's in business administration, she founded Leadership Solutions LLC, which is her platform "where issues become opportunities." She focuses on best practices that involve team building, employee management, conflict resolution, and effective HR practices. Christine's vision is to inspire businesses and individuals to reach their full potential by modifying behaviors and promoting change to reach maximum performances.

In addition, Christine has exhibited a proven track record of leadership excellence in her community. While serving as Parent Teacher Student Association (PTSA) president at Barbour County High School, she designed a scholarship program to help deserving young men and women to go to college. She also serves as the secretary of the Barbour County Quarterback Club, where many students have also gone to college from scholarship funds raised by volunteer efforts. She is a graduate of the 2009 Leadership Barbour Class III program, which is organized by the Barbour County Chamber of Commerce, where she served on the finance committee and serves as board member. Christine is a faithful member of Old Mt. Silla Missionary Baptist Church, where she serves as part of the intercessory, finance, and pastor aide ministries.

Christine believes that building human capital is the catalyst in building businesses. It is crucial that businesses invest in their people with effective training and ensure that clear, consistent practices are engrained in its culture. During her years as a human resources director, Christine found creative and motivational ways to teach management leadership principles by filtering messages through short stories, testimonies, and poems.

Christine lives in Clayton, Alabama, with her loving and supportive husband of twenty-three years, Patrick. She is a mother of two sets of twins, Tierra, Dierra, Jackita, and Larita, and grandmother of four.